# PAISLEY & MANDALA ANTI STRESS ADULT COLORING BOOK SETS

Copyright 2015

All Rights reserved. No part of this book may be reproduced or used in any way or form or by any means whether electronic or mechanical, this means that you cannot record or photocopy any material ideas or tips that are provided in this book.

*Cheryl Tabb*

**This Book Belongs To**

Bleed through page....Keep the stress away by coloring every day!

Bleed through page....Keep the stress away by coloring every day!

Bleed through page....Keep the stress away by coloring every day!

Bleed through page....Keep the stress away by coloring every day!

Bleed through page....Keep the stress away by coloring every day!

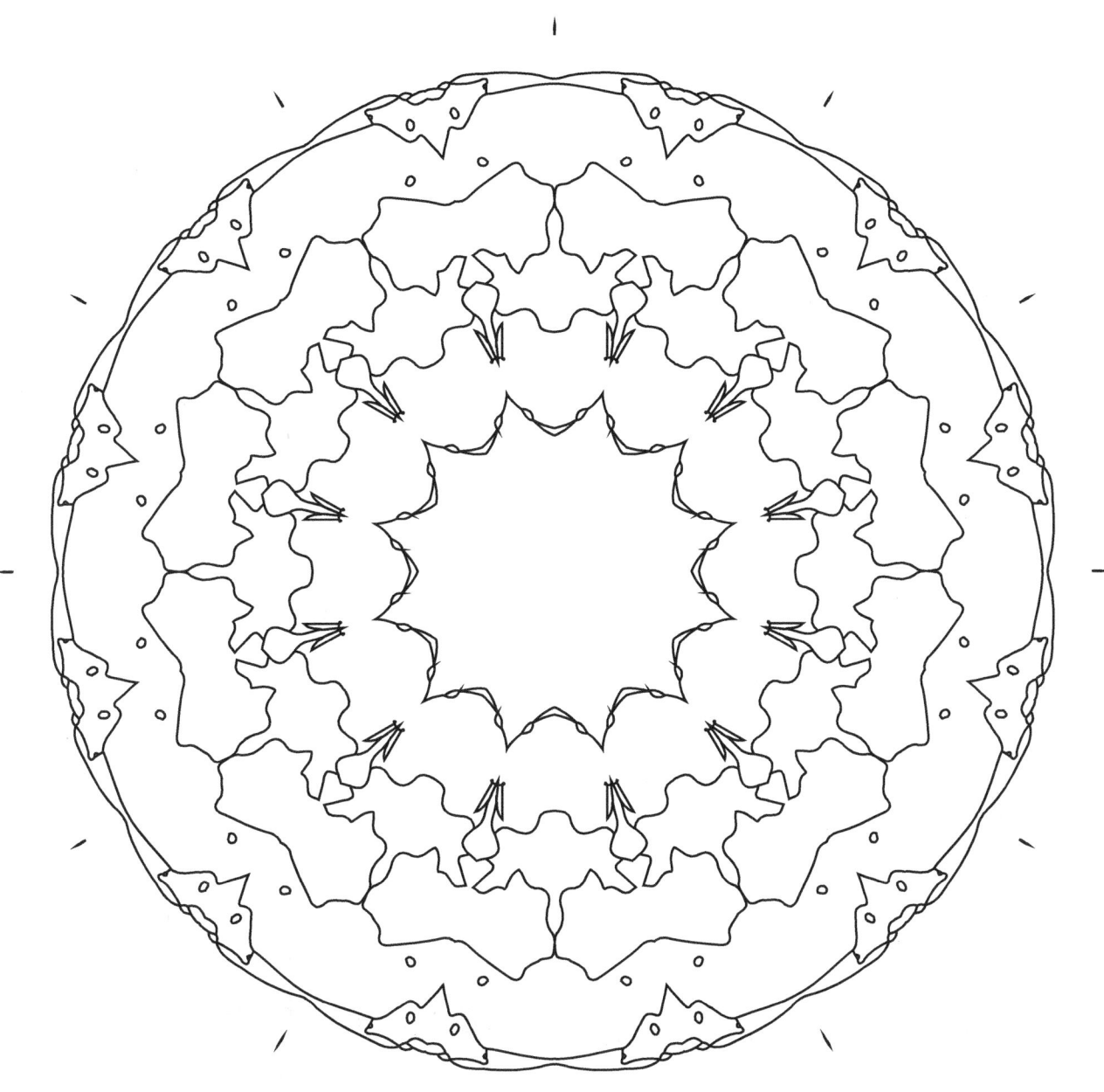

Bleed through page....Keep the stress away by coloring every day!

Bleed through page....Keep the stress away by coloring every day!

Bleed through page....Keep the stress away by coloring every day!

Bleed through page....Keep the stress away by coloring every day!

Bleed through page....Keep the stress away by coloring every day!

Bleed through page....Keep the stress away by coloring every day!

Bleed through page....Keep the stress away by coloring every day!

Bleed through page....Keep the stress away by coloring every day!

Bleed through page....Keep the stress away by coloring every day!

Bleed through page....Keep the stress away by coloring every day!

Bleed through page....Keep the stress away by coloring every day!

Bleed through page....Keep the stress away by coloring every day!

Bleed through page....Keep the stress away by coloring every day!

Bleed through page....Keep the stress away by coloring every day!

Bleed through page....Keep the stress away by coloring every day!

Bleed through page....Keep the stress away by coloring every day!

Bleed through page....Keep the stress away by coloring every day!

Bleed through page....Keep the stress away by coloring every day!

Bleed through page....Keep the stress away by coloring every day!

Bleed through page....Keep the stress away by coloring every day!

Bleed through page....Keep the stress away by coloring every day!

Bleed through page....Keep the stress away by coloring every day!

Bleed through page....Keep the stress away by coloring every day!

Bleed through page....Keep the stress away
by coloring every day!

Bleed through page....Keep the stress away by coloring every day!

Bleed through page....Keep the stress away by coloring every day!

Bleed through page....Keep the stress away by coloring every day!

Bleed through page....Keep the stress away by coloring every day!

Bleed through page....Keep the stress away by coloring every day!

Bleed through page....Keep the stress away by coloring every day!

Bleed through page....Keep the stress away by coloring every day!

Bleed through page....Keep the stress away by coloring every day!

Bleed through page....Keep the stress away by coloring every day!

Bleed through page....Keep the stress away by coloring every day!

Bleed through page....Keep the stress away by coloring every day!

Bleed through page....Keep the stress away by coloring every day!

Bleed through page....Keep the stress away by coloring every day!

Bleed through page....Keep the stress away by coloring every day!

Bleed through page....Keep the stress away by coloring every day!

Bleed through page....Keep the stress away by coloring every day!

Bleed through page....Keep the stress away by coloring every day!

Bleed through page....Keep the stress away by coloring every day!

Bleed through page....Keep the stress away by coloring every day!

Bleed through page....Keep the stress away by coloring every day!

Bleed through page....Keep the stress away by coloring every day!

CPSIA information can be obtained
at www.ICGtesting.com
Printed in the USA
BVHW012123050520
579267BV00013B/357